HOW TO TEACH REFERENCE AND RESEARCH SKILLS

FLORENCE V. SHANKMAN, Ed.D.

assistant professor of education, keene state college
keene, new hampshire

and

ROBERT KRANYIK, M.A.

assistant professor of education, university of bridgeport
formerly assistant principal oldfield school, fairfield, conn.

TEACHERS PRACTICAL PRESS, INC.

Robert L. Schain, Editor-in-Chief
Murray Polner, Associate Editor

The TEACHERS PRACTICAL PRESS, INC. subscribes to the philosophy that the key to good teaching is to be found in the quality of the teacher himself. This being the case, we recognize the great value and need for today's educator to develop and maintain a continuing program of professional self-improvement through the acquisition of up-to-date teaching techniques. This practical help can be gained only by becoming knowledgeable about practices and methods which have been found useful and successful.

Our goal is to provide this vital area of practical information for all educators. We hope that our series will contribute to the improvement of the teacher and teaching.

Address all inquiries to:
Atherton Press, 70 Fifth Avenue, New York 10011

Library of Congress Catalog Card Number: 63-15441

Copyright © Teachers Practical Press, Inc., 1964

CONTENTS

1

READING A SINGLE SELECTION

Here are some clues to the organization of material which can aid the student to formulate an image of the presentation.

1. The table of contents gives an overview of the contents and sequence of presentation of major ideas.

2. Introductory statements, prefaces, and forewords, which are often skipped by anxious readers, often give valuable clues to the nature of the presentation and the author's intent.

3. Summary chapters or paragraphs, if well written, can picture very concisely the nature of the content and its major conclusions.

4. The author's own conceptual outline of the subject matter is usually very evident if one examines main titles, subtitles, center headings and paragraph headings.

5. In historical materials, time-lines may sometimes be found which aid students in orienting themselves to a chronologically-developed presentation.

The setting of more specific purposes, or the formulating of questions to be answered during the reading can be set up during or after the initial survey of the material stressing the points mentioned above. There are two helpful approaches to such purpose or question formulation when purposes are subject to the internal organization of the text. The first consists of using as guides the author's headings—chapter headings, sub-headings, and paragraph headings. These may be turned into questions to be answered during the reading as in the example below:

Headings	Questions
The Cultural Matrix of Modern America [1]	What are the important ideas to remember about modern American culture?
Contributions of Immigrant Groups	What contributions did immigrants make to American culture?
Contributions of the Pioneer Movement	What contributions did the pioneer movement make to American culture?
The Effect of Technology upon the American Culture	How did the rise of technology affect the American culture? (in handwriting)

Questions concerning the material presented are often included at the ends of chapters. This is particularly true of textbooks. Students can often use such questions as jumping-off points in their attempts to read materials for study purposes. Thus, questions to which the answers are already known may be put aside, and concentration can be focused on those which present a real challenge. A good set of questions usually forces the student to review the material comprehensively.

▶ Efficient and rewarding reading

The initial survey of material and formulation of purposes or questions serve only as the beginning phase of effective study. The student must now apply himself to the task of finding valid, reliable, and relevant answers to his questions.

The author's style and use of words, phrases, and typographical devices are useful aids in extracting important ideas. For example, the student might be asked to identify such aids in the following paragraph and to indicate how they contribute to the understanding of important ideas.

---

[1] Special terms used in the presentation should be looked up in the glossary or in a dictionary if context clues are not adequate for the development of meaning.

Speed in miles per hour will not tell a pilot how near he is to the sonic barrier. For this reason, airplane speed is rated in a unit called the *Mach* (mock) in honor of a German scientist, Professor Ernst Mach, who was one of the pioneers in the study of supersonic speed. The speed in Machs is found by dividing the speed of air vibration at the plane's altitude by the plane's speed in miles per hour. Thus you will find that the sonic barrier is always rated as Mach 1.[2]

Often, particularly in science materials, complete operations and processes are described in the text and the descriptions are supplemented by diagrams, charts or graphs. Students should be taught to use such diagrams habitually since they are extremely valuable aids to comprehension. It is possible to illustrate the importance of such aids by exercises such as the following:

Ask the students to read the paragraph below and then to describe in their own words the functioning of a turbojet engine.

The Turbojet

Force from jets can also be obtained from the turbojet engine. In this type of engine, air is scooped in and compressed by a turbine-like compressor. This dense air is now used to burn the fuel in a combustion chamber. The resulting rapidly-expanding, high-pressure gases now pass through a gas turbine which turns the compressor. As they expand, they push on all points inside the engine except where they escape through the tailpipe, and force the plane to move forward. This engine operates most efficiently at high altitudes because the jet of exhaust

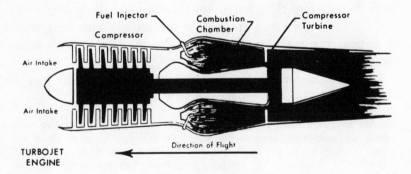

The turboprop engine is not so powerful as the turbojet. But it consumes less fuel and hence it is better for long-distance flying. Its weight is only about 1/2 pound per horsepower generated.

[2] Adapted from J. Darrell Barnard, Celia Stendler, and Benjamin Spock, *Science: A Key To the Future* (New York: The Macmillan Co., 1962), p. 125.

gases can escape with the least interference and thus develop the greatest amount of thrust possible. Thrust is the force which drives an airplane forward.[3]

An interesting variation is to ask the students to draw a diagram of the engine based on the description of the paragraph. When you are satisfied that they have done their best, show them the diagram reproduced on p. 7. Comparison with their own previous images or attempts to reproduce it should be enough to illustrate to them the value of pictorial presentations.

► Exercises to teach critical reading

Students working independently on reference or research projects should develop the skills needed to read material critically. Such skills include the ability to differentiate between fact and opinion, to evaluate the qualifications of the author to make the statements which appear, to detect the existence of bias or the use of emotionally toned words designed to elicit a favorable or unfavorable reaction from the reader, and to recognize the nature and use of various propaganda techniques often met in writing. These skills are most vital, not only to successful study, but to fruitful living in general, since many situations which are met in life contain elements of half-truth and bias, and it is well that students learn to recognize them early. Instruction and, above all, practice are important if students are to cope successfully with the problems of critical reading. Try these exercises to develop a functional understanding of the skills listed above.

1. The paragraph below contains elements of both fact and opinion. Underline the sentences which are opinion.

Moths and butterflies vary in size from less than the diameter of a dime to more than seven inches across their wings. Most of them live only a short while, although it is possible that some may live as long as three to five years. The wings of both butterflies and moths are covered on both sides with very tiny scales which are similar to those of the fish. It is felt that these scales may exist in order to provide protection to the wings on rainy days. Scientists tell us that butterflies and moths are the only insects which have wings covered with scales.

---

[3] Paragraph and illustration adapted from Bernard, Stendler, and Spock, p. 120.

2. You are interested in learning about the customs of Indians living in central Mexico. Which of the following persons do you think would be best qualified to make true statements about the above topic?

a. Mr. Smith is an oil company executive from Texas. He has been to Mexico City several times to visit business executives, and is a graduate of the state university where he studied geology.

b. Miss Long works for an art firm in New York City where she paints illustrations for children's books. Her latest work called for her to illustrate Mexicans at work and at play. In order for her to do an authentic job, she had to spend a great deal of time studying at the library. She also talked to a number of Mexicans at the United Nations.

c. Mr. Stetson is an anthropologist. An anthropologist is a person who studies about the lives of people in different parts of the world. He has lived with Indians in Central Mexico and has written a book about their customs.

d. Mrs. Wilkins is the wife of a medical doctor who once spent two years working with the Indians of Central Mexico. Over the years he has told his wife a great deal about his experiences with them. She has also read a great deal about them, although she has not yet been able to visit them.

Many ideas can be developed in this exercise, including the value of professional training, the validity of first hand experience, and the idea that qualifications can sometimes be relative, i.e., second hand experience, such as that of Miss Long's, can be accepted for certain purposes.

3. The following paragraph appeared in a local daily paper recently. It describes the new model sports car put on the market by a leading car manufacturer. Draw circles around the words and phrases which indicate a definite bias toward the new car.

Our new _____ model, which recently was placed on the market, has met with tremendous success. Everybody is just raving about its unprecedented beauty, its unmatched luxury, and its "he-man" power. It is truly a car for all the family; its sheer comfort and ease of handling make it a favorite for Mother when she makes those frequent shopping trips, its four speed transmission and giant sized V-8 engine spell "get away acceleration" for Father when he feels he needs the added safety of extra speed. Yes, everyone has a "Fourth of July" picnic driving the new ———————. Won't you join us?

4. Propaganda techniques take many forms including the following:

    a. *The Testimonial*—This is an attempt to sell a product or a cause by having a well-known person testify to the fact that he has used the product or believes in the cause.

    b. *The Use of Transfer*—This approach usually tries to gain acceptance for a product or a cause by suggesting a transfer of certain qualities of a well-known person to a product. Advertising often uses this approach when famous athletes or film stars are pictured with familiar products. The intent is to transfer the admiration for the person to the product.

    c. *The Glittering Generality*—Here the purpose is to convince people of the efficacy of a product or a cause by making sweeping, unsupported statements about it.

    d. *Name Calling*—Words which can arouse emotions are often used to affect people's attitudes in the absence of facts. Both negative and positive emotions can be aroused, depending upon the purpose.

    e. *The Bandwagon*—Often people are persuaded to make up their minds before examining the facts by the introduction into the situation of such moments as "Everybody's doing it" and "All of your neighbors are for it."

    f. *Card Stacking*—A one-sided argument can be very persuasive, particularly to the person who does not have insight into the situation. A series of facts may be presented to make a case for a cause or a product, but care is taken to include only favorable information. It is extremely difficult to see through this type of argument.

Below are some statements which make use of various propaganda techniques. Read each one carefully and try to identify the technique.

1. You really ought to read that new novel. It seems that everybody who is anybody has read it. You don't want to be left behind, do you?
2. Our fountain pens can write under water, on the desert, and even in the stratosphere. They come in more colors than any other pen on the market. Buy one today if you want the best.
3. The man is undemocratic. Why, he wouldn't even come out to talk with me when I went to see him about changing a few things around

here. He just said he was busy painting the garage door and had to finish before dark.

► *Enhancing retention and recall*

It is a good idea to spend a few minutes immediately after reading an article to review the material briefly. The questions which were formulated earlier should now be answered in writing. It is a well-known fact that recall is greatly improved by a self-check before putting the book down. Another check, a day or so later, will serve to clinch the new information.

2

USING MULTIPLE SOURCES

Using a variety of sources to secure information requires a number of skills in addition to those discussed previously. Students are often overwhelmed by the number and diversity of available resource materials. Thus, it is essential that clear and specific purposes be accompanied by a working knowledge of the *locational* skills. Other tasks which must be accomplished in successful reference work include the evaluation of material, its recording by means of appropriate techniques, and the organization of such material into a meaningful whole.

► Locational skills

These skills include the ability to use the library card catalogue, standard reference works, and to be familiar with the many sources of information available to today's students. There are very specific skills to be mastered in each of these areas. Please consult chapters 3, 4, 5 and 6 for specific techniques for the development of the above skills.

► Evaluation skills

As a student pores over his source material, he must make many decisions concerning the selection of specific items for his purposes. These decisions are best made when students are familiar with the criteria for evaluation and are able to apply them functionally. Exercises for the development of both an understanding and application of these criteria are presented below.

A. Using the Copyright Date

Many fields of knowledge, particularly science and the social studies, are subject to almost daily change as new discoveries are made and developments brought about. Sometimes it is only the daily newspaper which can give completely up-to-date facts and figures. There are some types of information that require recent books. Historical material may be as validly presented in older sources as in the latest book on the subject.

In the following exercise the students are asked to decide which types of information require a more careful check of the copyright date. It should be pointed out that this is often a relative matter and that at best, one accepts the best authority available. It is entirely possible in historical matters for new information to be obtained which may supersede previously well established facts, as in the case of the use of carbon dating and pollen analysis techniques in archaeology.

Read each of the topics below carefully and decide which of them would require a more intense check for recency through the use of copyright information.

1. The official proceedings of the Japanese surrender to Allied forces in the Pacific Theater of War in 1945.
2. The most accurate estimates of the surface temperature of the planet Venus.
3. The number of children under twelve attending school in Valparaiso, Chile.
4. The role of morality in the plays of William Shakespeare.
5. The effects of radiation upon the functioning of the human body in orbital flight.

Occasionally, it must be pointed out to students that textbooks and tradebooks have several copyright dates included, and that it is necessary to use the latest one for determining how recently the book was printed.

B. Determining the Relevance of the Information

In order to conserve time and energy, and to insure the continuity of ideas in reference work, the student should learn to select only material which relates directly to his purposes. Extraneous information should be rejected. Exercises such as the one below can be used to develop both the awareness and the skill needed to select information appropriate to the given topic or purpose.

The two paragraphs below, taken from different sources, contain information which may or may not be pertinent to the topic at hand. Underline sentences which you think contain information which can be used to develop the topic.

Topic—The *reason* rice is the major crop of Japanese agriculture.

Paragraph 1.

Many kinds of crops are grown in Japan, but rice is the leading one, and the chief food of the people. If you lived with a Japanese family, you would probably eat rice three times a day. You would have great fun in doing so too, because you would probably use chopsticks instead of a spoon or fork. Rice is a good crop for Japan because it provides so much food from each unit of farmland. More than half of all the land that can be planted for crops is planted in rice.[1]

Paragraph 2.

Rice is the most important food crop (of Japan). It grows well in the warm, damp climate of southern Japan. Even so, not enough rice is raised to feed Japan's growing population. A good deal must be imported. Wheat and millet are raised in the cool regions father north.[2]

C. COMPARING INFORMATION FROM SEVERAL SOURCES

The comparison of information from several sources to determine the extent of agreement or disagreement is a skill of considerable sophistication, and can challenge the most astute researcher. Often, ideas are couched in entirely different patterns of thought and expression, yet must be analyzed and sifted in order that valid generalizations may be drawn.

The first step in making such a comparison is the clear definition of the problem or proposition to be proven. This should be followed by the development of criteria for the analysis of information. The criteria should then be applied to each statement which appears to have relevance to the original problem.

In the exercise below, the problem has been defined and the criteria have been established. The student should examine each

---

[1] Adapted from Robert M. Glendinning, *Eurasia* (Boston: Ginn and Co.), p. 320.

[2] Adapted from Grace S. Dawson, *Your World and Mine* (Boston: Ginn and Co., 1960), p. 409.

statement in the light of the problem and the criteria and decide which statements tend to prove or disprove something, and to conclude whether or not the extent of the agreement is sufficient to warrant a conclusion.

Proposition: The availability of materials for construction has always been an important determining factor in the development of types of shelter used throughout the world by man.

Criteria: 1. Statements should refer to shelter created by man.
2. Statements should mention the idea that the availability of materials affected the type of shelter.

a. The Arabs of the Sahara Desert often live in houses made of bricks which they manufacture from mud dried in the sun. Such settlements are always located at oases which are scattered throughout the treeless, sandy desert.

b. The huge forests of Norway and Finland have, since Viking times, supplied the logs used in the construction of typical Scandinavian homes.

c. Most of the large buildings of Japanese cities are not constructed of concrete and steel in order to withstand the frequent earthquakes which plague that area of the world.

d. To the natives of many Pacific islands, the coconut palm which is found almost everywhere in the area is a staple of life, providing food, goods for trade, material for the construction of houses, and even eating utensils.

e. The Plains Indians of the United States lived for centuries on the treeless plains in tepees made of skins of animals and supported by long, narrow poles.

It should be noted that the matter of evidence is almost always subjective to some degree and that often the student must make his decision on the basis of the weight of evidence indicated by the statements which apply. In the above exercise a number of statements do apply, some having contemporary significance and others having historical significance. One of the statements (Statement "C") makes no reference to the availability of materials, and clearly does not serve to strengthen the proposition. The student should understand that the more evidence he is able to gather, the stronger the case he can build for his proposition. However, all evidence on both sides of the issue must be examined with an open mind; otherwise the danger of bias may enter.

15

▶ Recording information

Two approaches can be used to record information for future use, depending upon the needs of the student. When he is reading a single source for the purpose of acquiring understanding of the major ideas contained in it, the outline is perhaps most useful. In situations where multiple sources are used, the problem of organization becomes more complex, since materials are often organized in different ways. The use of index cards which can later be organized according to the reader's outline are recommended for this type of study.

A. OUTLINING A SINGLE SELECTION

In outlining a single selection, titles, subtitles, center heads, and paragraph heads can be used to form the framework of an outline, since they usually represent the author's own ideas on the organization of the content. Students should be given experiences in outlining chapters in textbooks or tradebooks by making use of such aids. Notice the logic and informational value of the material shown below. It was taken from a textbook now used in many schools.[3] In studying a chapter such as this, the student can simply enter the important ideas under each heading in note form and when he is finished, he has a very useful outline of the important information included in the chapter. Although only a portion of the chapter is shown here, the value of the headings should be obvious.

Brazil and Paraguay

I. Brazil.
  A. The Tropical Giant.
    1. A Few Comparisons.
      a. Largest country in Latin America.
      b. One of five largest countries in world.
      c. Only large tropical country.
    2. A Giant in Area, but Not in Population.
      a. About same size as U.S.
      b. One-third as U.S. in population.
      c. Most people live near Atlantic Coast.

---

[3] Adapted from Katheryn Whittemore, Marguerite Uttley, and Alison E. Aitchison, *United States, Canada, and Latin America* (Boston: Ginn and Co., 1962), pp. 447-452.

3. Brazil on the March.
    a. Westward movement taking place.
    b. Economic progress being made.
B. East Central Brazil.
    1. A Crowded Region.
        a. Nearly half of Brazilian population lives here.
        b. Two largest cities located here.

B. Note-Taking from Multiple Selections

When a student is working with multiple selections or sources, he usually has in mind an outline which he has developed. The information needed to supply the body of the project must come from the materials with which he is working. He needs a method of approach which will help him in a number of ways, including:

   a. Ease in moving from the organizational structure of one source to that of another.
   b. Ease in organizing the information obtained from multiple sources into a form which fits his needs.
   c. Adequate space for recording all essential information.
   d. Ready identification of each citation for footnoting and bibliographical purposes.

▶ Using index cards

The following method can accomplish all of these goals, and can be used at various levels with appropriate modifications. The use of index cards is recommended in the multiple source approach, since they are easy to handle and can be rearranged quickly. The 3 by 5 lined card is adequate for some types of reference work although the 5 by 8 card is much more useful when more involved material is being examined. Each card should be limited to one source and one idea contained in that source. The upper left hand corner of the card should contain the proper bibliographical information such as author, title, edition, publisher, date of copyright, page numbers, etc. On additional cards citing from the same work, only the name of the author and the work need be cited. The page from which the information is taken can be written in the left-hand margin, and since several pages in a work may contain information

17

relative to the same idea, each new inclusion can be readily identified by the page number. For an involved reference project, the cards can be numbered according to the outline developed by the student, with the number being placed in the upper right hand corner. It is also helpful to give each card a title which shows at a glance the nature of the material recorded on it. Another helpful approach to complex research work is to construct a small file box for the cards and to divide it into sections according to the student's outline. Cards may be turned vertically and major headings written on them. Colored tabs or other forms of coding may also be used. Well-organized notes allow the student to write his final document with much less confusion and will preclude a great deal of frustration.

A SAMPLE NOTE CARD [4]

Wright, Franklin	I-A-3
Economics of the Western Hemisphere	
N.Y.: Smith and Co., 1963, pp. 421	

Major Economic Problems (major category)

p. 42 Major economic problems include the rise of automation, changes in world markets, and the dollar flow from the U.S.

p. 52 Rise of European common market has resulted in competition in areas previously limited to U.S. products.

p. 71 Nationalization policies of many nations have inhibited the investment of U.S. capital overseas.

Additional index cards referring to this same source of information would be listed as follows:

Wright—*Econ. of the W. Hemisphere* (students could work out their own abbreviations for titles, e.g.—Wright, or EWH, etc.)

After the student has completed his use of reference materials, and notes have been written on index cards, he should then arrange these cards in the order indicated by his subject outline and insert them into the file box. The actual presentation (orally or in writing) of the project then merely becomes a matter of putting the gathered

---

[4] This card is completely fictitious and is being used for illustrative purposes only. The student's notes may be either printed or written.

information in continuous form. Experience has shown that this method of organizing research notes has made the student's job easier and has produced a better product. Training in this phase of research skills early in the student's schooling will make his work in the upper grades considerably better.

3

TEACHING STUDENTS TO USE DICTIONARIES

Few teachers realize fully the fact that a dictionary, even a simplified children's edition, is a veritable treasure house of information. It is one of the most useful tools that the elementary child has at his fingertips. The dictionary contains information about a wide range of topics. It is possible to find the life size of an iguana, the value of a florin in American money, or the colors of the Brazilian flag. The contributions to the development of verbal skills are, of course, immense. Its value as a leavening tool should be constantly stressed and the development of proper techniques for its use should be continuously fostered.

For young children in the primary grades a number of picture dictionaries have appeared during the past few years. These are especially valuable for the development of a positive attitude toward the use of the dictionary as a tool. The format used in most picture dictionaries is similar to that of more advanced works, except that it is usually kept quite simple and makes extended use of pictures to aid in the acquisition of word meanings. Such pictures contribute much to the child's attempt to use the dictionary independently to locate words, acquire meanings, and apply both spellings and meanings in written work.

Secondary level students should become proficient in the use of unabridged dictionaries, for they provide many types of information not included in simplified editions, such as the foreign origins for words, exact meanings of synonyms, and the identification of obsolete words.

▶ Skill development in dictionary use

Perhaps the most effective means to skill development in dictionary use is formal teaching of the necessary skills in a sequential pattern with ample opportunity for application in meaningful situations. Each lesson should present and develop a skill or series of skills. During such lessons the students should actually *use* the dictionary, and if possible, should relate their findings to areas of interest in the content fields.

The following exercises are illustrations of the types of activities which can be included in a program designed to improve dictionary use. As sample exercises, they may be used as guides to develop other exercises related to specific dictionaries found in the classroom. Such exercises may function as developmental lessons as well as evaluative devices to determine the degree of proficiency which has been attained.

1. *The Alphabetical Order of Things*

In order to locate a word which you are seeking, it is important to know the first letter, or in some cases the first two or three letters, since the dictionary is arranged in alphabetical order. The following exercise will help you to review alphabetical order.

Can you say the alphabet? Which comes first "n" or "t," "h" or "g"? What comes before m,w,k? What comes after s,e,q? Place these words in alphabetical order:

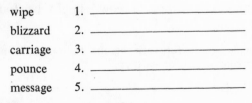

wipe	1. _____
blizzard	2. _____
carriage	3. _____
pounce	4. _____
message	5. _____

animals   6. _____

known   7. _____

yard   8. _____

Do you remember the rule for alphabetizing words which begin with the same letter? Try placing these words in alphabetical order.

barb	1. _____	flicker	1. _____
boom	2. _____	flint	2. _____
band	3. _____	fleece	3. _____
bedroom	4. _____	flame	4. _____
bitter	5. _____	fly	5. _____

2. *Using the Quarter System*

It is possible to locate words much faster if you think of the dictionary as being divided into four quarters as described below. If you wish to find a word, think about the quarter which contains the letter with which it begins. Open to that quarter. The word which you are looking for will not be far from the page to which you opened if you have estimated correctly. Here are the quarters:

| *First Quarter* | *Second Quarter* | *Third Quarter* | *Fouth Quarter* |
| ABCD | EFGHIJKL | MNOPQR | STUVWXYZ |

To which quarter would you turn to locate the following words?

labor _____   huge _____   popularity _____

colorful _____   unsanitary _____   equipment _____

welfare _____   anxious _____   newcomers _____

3. *Guide Words*

Guide words at the top of each page give us clues about the words located on the page. Since the guide words are the first and last words on the page, the word you are looking for should be located between the guide words, if it is to be found on the page at all. For example, the word "follow" might be found between "fodder" and "fondly."

Write the guide words for each of the following. Remember that there are two guide words on each page.

gerund _____   _____

mend _____   _____

restore _____ _____

garble _____ _____

witty _____ _____

4. *Key Words*

Key words give us clues to the pronunciation of words. Each dictionary has its own set of key words although they are basically similar. Key words which would help us to pronounce the word "partner" might be "hard" and "letter." The "ar" sound is *hard* and the "er" sound in *letter* tell us how to pronounce the vowel sounds in *partner*.

The different kinds of marks found over letters are called diacritical marks. They help us to find the key words. For example, if the word we are working with is "pastry" (pas′ tri), the key words "able" and "if" can be easily located by looking for the diacritical marks.

Find the key words for each of the following:

pattern	(pat ern)	1. _____	2. _____
rhizome	(ri zom)	1. _____	2. _____
tepid	(tep id)	1. _____	2. _____
equate	(e kwat)	1. _____	2. _____
Worcester	(Woos ter)	1. _____	2. _____

5. *Preferred Pronunciation*

Many words are pronounced in two ways. The dictionary tells us which is the preferred pronunciation. Find the preferred pronunciation of each of these words. Circle it.

truculent	trŭk′ŭ lĕnt	trōō′kŭ lĕnt
pretense	prē̆ tĕns′	prē′ tĕns
rodeo	rō dā′ō	rō′dē̆ ō
cocaine	kō′kān	kō kān′
Lombardy	Lŏm′ bẽr di	Lŭm′ bẽr di

6. *Parts of Speech*

At times you may wish to find the part of speech of a word. The dictionary will often tell you which part of speech a word is by listing an abbreviation after the word such as n. for noun, v. for verb, etc. Use your dictionary to find which part of speech may be used to classify each word below:

nastiness _____

toxic _____

legend _____

lustily _____

allot _____

6. *Different Meanings of a Word*

A dictionary often gives a number of meanings of a word. You can tell which meaning to choose by the way the word is used in a sentence. Give the meaning of each underlined word in the sentences below by choosing the appropriate meaning from the dictionary.

1. There was a *canopy* over the entrance. _____
2. He cleaned the *jet* on the new gas stove. _____
3. Sweet potatoes contain a great deal of *starch*. _____
4. The money was kept in this *vault*. _____
5. He stood at the *bar* and said, "I am not guilty." _____

7. *Interesting Information*

A dictionary can give us many interesting items of information. Answer each of the following questions by using any part of your dictionary.

1. Why was Franz Liszt famous? _____
2. When did Mary Stuart live? _____
3. How long generally is a peccary from nose to tail? _____
4. What does the abbreviation N.A.S. stand for? _____
5. Which is the correct abbreviation for Florida, Flor. or Fla.? _____
6. How long generally is a meadow lark from bill to tail (in inches)?

   _____

7. Give a synonym for each of the following words:

   salute _____ fete_____
8. How many feet are in a nautical mile? _____ In metric measure, one kilometer equals how many meters? _____

24

9. People in Iceland use the ———————————— as a unit of money while in Uruguay the ———————————— is used.

10. Which state has more people, Alabama or Connecticut? ————————

11. Which has a larger population, Athens, Greece, or Cologne, Germany? ————————————

12. In astronomy the symbol ♄ stands for ———————————, while in commerce ♃ stands for ————————————.

13. Write the name of the country to which each flag below belongs:

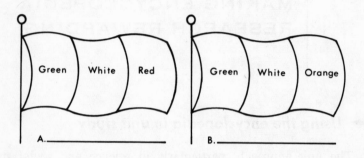

A.————————————   B.————————————

4

MAKING ENCYCLOPEDIA RESEARCH REWARDING

▶ Using the encyclopedia in unit study

The unit approach, particularly in science and social studies, offers many opportunities for use of the encyclopedia. Some suggestions for the integration of the encyclopedia with the total unit approach are given below. Although specifically oriented to the intermediate grades, such an integration is applicable at most levels.

Steps in Unit Study	*Functions of the Encyclopedia*
1. Orientation—The students gain an overview of the topic.	Used to supplement the textbook, bulletin boards, films, and other devices which contribute to a broad overview. Its comprehensive treatment aids in "filling in the gaps."
2. Formulation of Goals—The students submit questions and delineate major goals for unit study, with the help of the teacher.	A general survey of the topic encourages questioning and stimulates curiosity. Goals dealing with both facts and generalizations may be formulated through the use of encyclopedia information. Structured presentations aid the students in the formulation of their own worthwhile goals.
3. Organization of the Unit—The students and teacher outline the	The organization of topic treatment in the encyclopedia is so

26

major content areas and activities appropriate to learning in the content areas.

structured as to emphasize important areas.

4. Exploratory Activities — The students seek information related to their problems and questions under the guidance of the teacher.

The rich detail found in the encyclopedia provides answers to many questions, solves a number of problems. Cross references are keys to further information which, in turn, may answer other questions.

5. Assimilating Activities — The students present information to the entire group, discuss it, and then record it in appropriate form.

The illustrations, charts, graphs, and maps found in encyclopedias serve as examples of ways in which information may be pictorially recorded.

6. Unit Culmination—The students summarize what they have learned, select an activity or medium to demonstrate the importance and relatedness of their learnings, and evaluate the success of the unit. The teacher may evaluate the growth of the students.

Some encyclopedias suggest activities which may be used as culminating activities. Material from the encyclopedias may be used along with that gathered from other sources for the creation of evaluative instruments.

► **Developing skills for effective use of the encyclopedia**

1. *Locating information organized in alphabetical order.*

   a. In which volume of the set of encyclopedias illustrated below would you find each of the following topics?

   aviation _____   Kansas _____   Time _____
   zebra _____   elevators _____   rockets _____

A	B	C	D	E	F	G	H	I	JK	L	M	NO	P	QR	S	T	UV	WX YZ
1	2	3	4	5	6	7	8	9	10	11	12	13	14	15	16	17	18	19

   b. Number each group of topics in the order in which you think they would appear in the encyclopedia.

————	Alaska	————	France	————	owl
————	Andes	————	fingerprints	————	oyster
————	Azores	————	flounder	————	octopus
————	Atlantic	————	Fahrenheit	————	otter

2. *Identifying key words of a topic.*

In order to locate information about a certain topic it is important to be able to identify key words which may be mentioned in the encyclopedia. Information about the topic may often be found under these key words. Underline the key words in each topic listed below.

Men of Ancient Times   The Defeat of Cornwallis at Yorktown
Legends of Old Mexico   Galileo and His Telescope

3. *Clarifying and limiting a topic.*

Often students have difficulty in finding information about a topic because it is too broad, and they have not identified specific questions which they wish to answer or have not set definite goals which they wish to achieve. The topic should be well thought out beforehand, and aspects to be singled out for study should be determined in advance. In planning your study of a topic, use the form presented below. It will help you to organize your own thoughts about the subject.

PROJECT GUIDE

Name————————————————————

My topic is————————————————————————

    I want to learn more about these aspects of my topic:

       a. ————————————————————————————

       b. ————————————————————————————

       c. ————————————————————————————

       d. ————————————————————————————

---

4. *Using a cross reference.*

The basic concept of the cross reference may be developed during lessons dealing with the index. Specific cross references located in an index usually refer to pages contained in the same book; those given in the encyclopedia often require the use of other volumes in the set. This distinction should be made clear to students.

Actual practice with encyclopedias is the most effective way to develop speed and efficiency in the use of cross references. The exercise below may also be of help in developing this skill.

Suppose you have located each of the following topics and notice that further information is available elsewhere as indicated by the cross references. Using the set of encyclopedias illustrated before, give the number of the volume in which you would find further information about each topic:——Pineapples (see Hawaiian Islands);——Welland Canal (see Great Lakes);——Aztecs (see Montezuma);——Churchill (see Great Britain).

5. *Using Reference Outlines and Other Indexes.*

Most encyclopedias contain some type of index, either at the end of each volume, or in a separate volume at the end of the set. The following reference outline is included to illustrate how it might be used to aid students in locating information, as well as to serve as a suggested outline of a topic.

REFERENCE OUTLINE FOR STUDY OF AVIATION AND
RELATED ARTICLES

THE AIR AGE [1]

I. Aviation affects all daily living A-596.
   A. Economic A-506-597.
   B. Transportation, communication, A-597-597 a-b, 598, A-91-2, T-190, map A-597-A, airmail A-91b.
   C. Military vigilance A-599, A-57, C-366a.
   D. Recreation A-598; model building A-111-13.
   E. Education A-598; Air Force Academy A-89-90.
   F. Language and literature A-598; aviation and areonautics terms, table (Fact Index).

Answer the following questions by placing the correct volume and page in the space beside each question.
   1. Where would you find information about building a flying model of a fighter? _____
   2. Where could you find out what a strut is used for? _____
   3. Where would you look to find out how airplanes help our country to grow? _____
   4. Where would you find out how to qualify as an air cadet at the Air Force Academy? _____
   5. Where might you find a map of important American air routes? _____

[1] Portion of a comprehensive reference outline found in *Compton's Pictured Encyclopedia.* Used by permission of F. S. Compton and Co., Chicago, Ill.

6. If your topic for research happened to be "The Importance of Aviation to Us," what would be some of the important sub-headings? Use the above index for suggestions.

1. _____ 2. _____ 3. _____

6. *Adjustment of Reading Rate to the Task at Hand.*

Efficient use of the encyclopedia calls for several types of reading. Skimming is useful when articles are being scanned for information. Slow, careful reading is called for when significant passages are being read. Important items of information which should be retained may often have to be reread several times in order for the student to extract the full meaning. These skills should be developed during the reading period, and applied in content situations using the encyclopedia.

5

TEACHING LIBRARY SKILLS

▶ Using your school library

Some suggestions for making better use of the school library are presented below: [1]

1. Become familiar with your school library. Make a habit of reading new additions from time to time so that you will be in a better position to guide your students in their selection of reading materials.

2. Keep the school librarian informed of your major projects and units so that she may provide materials to meet the needs of your students.

3. School librarians are often well trained in techniques for library use. Work cooperatively with the librarian to develop the skills and techniques needed by students when working in the library.

4. Often, teachers are invited to take part in the selection of books for the school library. Take advantage of this situation if it exists in your school. Your experiences with the students should aid you in making choices related to the needs, abilities and interests which they have.

[1] Grateful acknowledgment is made to Ruth Wallad, librarian of Thomas Jefferson High School, Brooklyn, New York, for her assistance in gathering the information for the Dewey Decimal System and the section on reference books in this chapter.

31

► Developing basic library skills

There are a number of skills considered essential to efficient use of the library. Many of these are discussed elsewhere in this book. Those especially related to library work are presented below.

1. Students should become familiar with the arrangement of books in the library and should develop the ability to locate books throughout the library. Books in the school library are arranged in a number of ways, according to type. Fiction is usually arranged in alphabetical order, by author's last names. Biographies are arranged alphabetically according to the last name of the subject. Many times there will be additional identification marks on the covers to indicate the reading level. For example, "E" may indicate an easy reader, one which a first or second grader would enjoy without great difficulty. Non-fiction books are arranged according to the Dewey Decimal System. Standard reference works such as encyclopedias, atlases, and almanacs are usually placed in a special reference section where they are arranged by alphabetical order within categories and sets, except for chronological arrangement when appropriate.

Activity—Take the class to the library and point out the location of various types of books while describing them. Prepare a number of 3 x 5 cards by writing on each the title of the book, name of the author, and the type of book (fiction, biography, etc.) Let each student choose a card at random and locate the specified book. As students search for their books, care should be taken to aid those who experience difficulty. When all of the books have been located, they should be redistributed to others for return to the shelves. In this way, learning is reinforced and the librarian is spared the additional work of replacing the book.

2. Students should become familiar with the Dewey Decimal System and develop skill in its use. The Dewey Decimal System was created by Melvil Dewey for the purpose of organizing non-fiction books according to subject categories.

Activities—Several filmstrips concerning the Dewey Decimal System are available for classroom use. One of these might be shown prior to a visit to the library. A visit should then be arranged with the school librarian to give the students further instruction and experience in using the system. If the librarian is not available, the following activity might be used with the students by the classroom teacher:

Divide a number of blank white cards into two groups. On each of the cards in the first group, write the classification number of a volume located in the library. (Remember that the classification at the elementary level is kept rather simple, while the secondary student should become thoroughly familiar with the adult system.) On the second group of cards, write the titles of several books located in the library. Let each student take two cards, one from each group, try to locate a volume by number, and find the number of a given title.

3. Students should gain familiarity with the card catalog and skill in its use to locate books in the library. Every school library should have a card catalog to aid the students in their search for particular books, to ascertain the number and types of books available on a given topic, and to allow children to find the number of books written by the same author. There are three types of catalog cards which students need to know about. They are illustrated below: [2]

These cards, arranged in alphabetical order, permit the student to locate a book in a number of ways:

1. Use of the author card to find the books written by a particular author.
2. Use of the title card if the title of the book is known.
3. Use of the subject card to locate books concerned with specific subject areas. Such books may be listed under several subject headings.

Activity—The following sample questions can be used to develop facility in the interpretation of catalogue cards. They refer specifically to the cards illustrated below.

1. What is the Dewey Decimal classification of the book *Space Book For Young People*? _____
2. Who is the author of this book? _____ When was he born? or How old is he? _____
3. Would you find any maps or pictures in this book? _____
4. Below are listed a number of topics about which you might like to locate information. After reading the summary of the book *Space Book For Young Children,* decide which of the topics might might be mentioned in the book. Write *yes* or *no* after each topic.
   a. Learning More About Comets _____
   b. Exploration Beneath the Sea _____
   c. Understanding Three-Stage Rockets _____
   d. Orbiting Space Stations _____
   e. Manufacturing Telescopes _____
5. If you did not know the title of the above book, where else in the catalog would you look to locate it?

---

[2] Reproduced by permission of H. W. Wilson Co., New York, N. Y.

1. Author Card

629.4 **Newell, Homer Edward,** 1915-
> Space book for young people. Rev. ed. Illus. by Anne Marie Jauss. McGraw 1960
> 128p illus maps (Whittlesey House publications)
>
>> First published 1958. The 1960 edition has been revised to bring it up-to-date and expanded to include new material on artificial satellites and rockets
>> "An authoritative . . . discussion of the earth and its relation to the universe, and of rockets, artificial satellites, rocket flight, and the exploration of space." Booklist
>
> 1 Astronomy 2 Space flight I Title   629.4
>
> 60W8,957   ◯   (W) The H. W. Wilson Company

2. Title Card

Space book for young people

629.4 **Newell, Homer Edward,** 1915-
> Space book for young people. Rev. ed. Illus. by Anne Marie Jauss. McGraw 1960
> 128p illus maps (Whittlesey House publications)
>
>> First published 1958. The 1960 edition has been revised to bring it up-to-date and expanded to include new material on artificial satellites and rockets
>> "An authoritative . . . discussion of the earth and its relation to the universe, and of rockets, artificial satellites, rocket flight, and the exploration of space." Booklist
>
> 1 Astronomy 2 Space flight I Title   629.4
>
> 60W8,957   ◯   (W) The H. W. Wilson Company

3. Subject Cards
a. Astronomy

ASTRONOMY

629.4   **Newell, Homer Edward,** 1915-

Space book for young people. Rev. ed. Illus. by Anne
Marie Jauss. McGraw 1960

128p illus maps (Whittlesey House publications)

First published 1958. The 1960 edition has been revised to bring it
up-to-date and expanded to include new material on artificial satellites
and rockets

"An authoritative . . . discussion of the earth and its relation to the
universe, and of rockets, artificial satellites, rocket flight, and the
exploration of space." Booklist

1 Astronomy   2 Space flight   i Title   629.4

60W8,957   (W)   The H. W. Wilson Company

---

b. Space Flight

SPACE FLIGHT

629.4   **Newell, Homer Edward,** 1915-

Space book for young people. Rev. ed. Illus. by Anne
Marie Jauss. McGraw 1960

128p illus maps (Whittlesey House publications)

First published 1958. The 1960 edition has been revised to bring it
up-to-date and expanded to include new material on artificial satellites
and rockets

"An authoritative . . . discussion of the earth and its relation to the
universe, and of rockets, artificial satellites, rocket flight, and the
exploration of space." Booklist

1 Astronomy   2 Space flight   i Title   629.4

60W8,957   (W)   The H. W. Wilson Company

---

4. Students should be introduced to the various types of indexes to biographies, poetry, and the like. An example of this is: *Biography Index,* New York: H. W. Wilson Co. A sample entry from the *Biography Index* is presented below: [3]

> LeMay, Curtis Emerson 1906—general New A.F. Chief por *Newsweek* 57:32-3, Je '61 New air chief por *Time* 77:19 Je 2 '61 People of the Week por *U.S. News* 50:27 Je 5 '61

Activity—The sample exercise below might be used with the students to develop proficiency in the use of index entries.
1. What is Curtis LeMay's occupation? ⎯⎯⎯⎯⎯
2. When was he born? (or how old is he?) ⎯⎯⎯⎯⎯
3. List three magazines in which you might find articles about him? ⎯⎯⎯⎯⎯, ⎯⎯⎯⎯⎯, ⎯⎯⎯⎯⎯
4. All of these articles were published in the month of ⎯⎯⎯⎯⎯, 19⎯.
5. On which page of *U.S. News and World Report* would you find the article entitled "People of the Week?" ⎯⎯⎯⎯⎯

There are also a number of specialized indexes that might be of value to students engaged in reference and research. Some of these are as follows:

Education Index—lists articles pertaining to education that have appeared in professional magazines.

Business Periodicals Index—indexes about 120 periodicals in the fields of accounting, banking, insurance, management, taxation, etc.

Applied Science and Technology Index—indexes about 200 periodicals in the fields of aeronautics, automation, chemistry, construction, engineering, machinery, and related subjects.

Psychological Abstracts—a monthly bibliography listing new books and articles grouped by subjects with a signed abstract of each item.

New York Times Index—This is an index of all news items that have appeared in *The New York Times.*

5. Students should gain proficiency in locating and using current materials in the library. The *Readers' Guide To Periodical Literature* by H. W. Wilson Co. is one of the most helpful aids to students who wish to make use of current materials in the library. There are two editions, the unabridged edition which is usually found in large libraries, and the abridged editions usually found

---

[3] Reproduced by permission of H. W. Wilson Co., New York, N. Y.

in smaller libraries and children's libraries. In both editions the topics are arranged in alphabetical order and are cross referenced. Note the sample entry below: [4]

ECLIPSES, Solar

> February's solar eclipse and the West Coast Sky and Tel 23:3 Ja '62

> Weather prospects for the eclipse in February EgM. Brooks il Sky and Tel 22:318-19 D'61

Activity—Students might be given a list of articles or topics listed in the *Readers' Guide* and asked to answer questions similar to the following by actually using the guide in the library.

1. What is the title of the magazine in which you would find articles about February's solar eclipse? (If they have difficulty with the title, ask them to refer to the list of titles at the front of the guide.)
   _____
2. Which article has an illustration? _____
3. Which article would seem to be the more general one? _____
4. Which of the two articles is of greater length? _____

► Introducing students to the public library

A teacher should encourage the use of the public library by her students, and coordinate, whenever possible, the learning activities of the school with the facilities and resources of the public library. Perhaps the following suggestions may be of value in encouraging better use of the public library:

• Stress the fact that the librarian can be helpful. Librarians often complain that people do not make adequate use of their services.

• Be familiar with the numerous types of resources available at the public library. Many libraries provide records, paintings, a research service, and book talks for both students and adults, in addition to the usual resources.

• If you are planning to assign a project to the class which will create a "rush" on certain types of books at the public library, it is a good idea to call the librarian ahead of time. This gives the librarian an opportunity to collect the books and have them ready and on reserve for your group.

---

[4] Reproduced by permission of H. W. Wilson Co., New York, N. Y.

• Arrange for your local library to send you listings of new additions to their shelves, if possible. These may be discussed with the students or posted for further reference.

• Take your students to the library. Introduce them to the librarian and ask her to familiarize them with the physical layout, regulations, and available resources. This should prevent much frustration on the part of both librarian and students.

6

USING AUDIO-VISUAL MATERIALS

▶ Using maps and globes

Skills needed for the effective use of maps and globes as aids in both study situations and reference work are of two types—*reading* skills and *interpretation* skills.

Reading skills include the knowledge of symbols, terms, colors, and other keys to finding one's way around maps and globes. The reading skills may be compared to the recognition by the reader of a book of letters, sentences, and paragraphs in his attempts to cope with the printed page.

Meaning, however, comes through interpretation. In map work, this refers to the ability to draw inferences from the study of the symbols as they appear on a map. Students should learn to interpret maps in terms of their previous experiences and in combination with textual materials. For example, from his past experience a student usually knows what conditions must be existent for successful farming, e.g., fairly fertile land which is reasonably level, favorable temperature ranges, and adequate rainfall. After studying a map of a particular region closely, he should be able to infer from the altitude of the land, or from its conformation, whether or not it might be suitable for farming. However, a more sophisticated and conclusive inference might better be drawn from the examination of several maps. Topographical maps give valuable information concerning land forms; climate maps delineate temperature ranges, and rainfall maps indicate whether or not sufficient moisture is available for agriculture. Population maps are also helpful since an agricultural region is not usually heavily populated, although it must be close to markets. Soil maps, land usage maps, and many other types can also contribute to a clearer understanding of our problem. It is important that students be introduced to the values of maps, that they learn to read and interpret many different kinds of maps, and that they use them in conjunction with printed materials for the purpose of gaining a clearer understanding of the world around them.

▶ Exercises to sharpen map and globe study

The exercise suggested below can point out to the student the important function of maps and globes in study situations. It should be preceded by instruction in map reading and the use of various types of atlases and globes.

Develop a problem which interests the students. It might range from "What kinds of work would people in Sweden do?" to "Why did the Japanese become an industrial nation over the past decades?"

Tell them that they must seek the answers to their questions from maps and globes only. Give them an opportunity to examine as many of these as they feel necessary, and then ask them to list their answers and the reasons for their answers. After this has been done, they may then check their answers by examining written materials. They will probably find that maps and globes helped them a great deal, and that these are valuable tools which should be consulted. However, there will doubtless be other conclusions and reasons for those conclusions which are not immediately evident from the maps, such as cultural factors and historical accidents. Thus they learn that maps and globes may best be used in combination with other materials.

▶ Using graphs

Students should be led to understand that graphs are pictorial representations of quantitative data, developed for the purpose of effecting a quick yet comprehensive understanding of complex concepts or operations. There are several types of graphs with which students should become familiar that include line graphs, bar graphs, picture graphs and circle graphs. It is important that students learn to use graphs functionally as aids to study. There are several types of skills needed for functional usage.

1. What does a brief survey of the graph tell us about the subject being portrayed, the type of information given, and the symbols used in the presentation?

2. How do we go about obtaining information from the graph?

3. Is more than one type of information given on the graph? Can comparisons of information be made on the graph? Can trends of various types be identified from the graph?

Let us examine the following graph in terms of the above questions. This graph is taken from an elementary social studies textbook.[1]

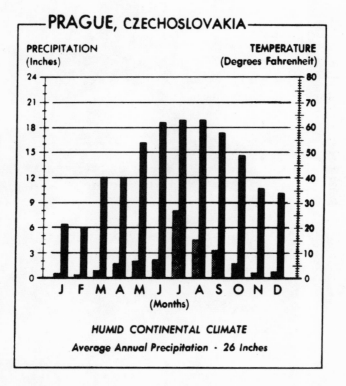

[1] Reproduced from Robert M. Glendinning, *Eurasia* (Boston: Ginn and Co., 1958), p. 172.

1. What is the topic of the above graph?
2. Define the following terms: precipitation, Fahrenheit, average?
3. What types of information does the graph give?
4. Which month of the year would ordinarily be most uncomfortable to a person who does not like extreme humidity?
5. When does the highest average annual temperature occur in Czechoslovakia?
6. Can you tell from looking at the graph whether Czechoslovakia is in the northern or southern hemisphere? In order to answer this question, what must you know about the seasons in each hemisphere?

7

TEACHING BASIC
RESEARCH TECHNIQUES

Topics or subjects for investigation arise when a student is aroused or excited by what he hears, sees or reads. Learning can be a very stimulating process that may start at any age. Ultimately, it must involve a definite purpose and plan of action, the ability to use the library, and the ability to convey the information to others in oral or written form. The individual should be interested in the problem if he expects to concentrate on the task or convince others. However, teachers are obligated to provide training in research skills even if intrinsic interest is not present. If students learn these basic skills in their school years, they will be equipped to apply them as adults when individual and community problems become more significant to them. The topic for investigation can be set up as a problem or question so that it can be handled in a limited amount of time and space. This may be clarified after a general discussion or after some reading on the topic.

▶ *Locating the information*

For example, most children are interested in weather reports. These may determine how they should dress, or in what activities they will participate for their play period. Most children have heard weather reports given over the radio or television as part of the news broadcasts. They may have heard discussions on some of the space flights and the part that weather has played in sending man into space. Children in many primary grades are taught to indicate the weather on a calendar, to learn to associate symbols for certain words or facts. If there is a difference of opinion, they are encouraged to verify the information by observing what is happening, by telling where they got the information, e.g., on radio, on television. Some children may bring in the printed report from a newspaper or tell what an adult may have said. These discussions can lead to training in critical thinking and to finding various sources of information. Children soon learn that books, magazines, and newspapers may provide us with information. How to locate the printed information that can be helpful leads to the use of the card catalogue, the index, various references such as the encyclopedia, maps, atlases, and biographical dictionaries.

► Analyzing the information

After the information has been located, the student should be able to separate the main ideas from the subordinate details, recognize the topic sentence, choose key words to express the major facts he wants to remember or use in his final report. How to make a bibliography can be introduced in the primary grades as soon as the child is aware of the fact that information can be obtained from more than one source. If he has been introduced to alphabetizing in order to locate a word in a dictionary, or to use an index, he can be taught to make a simple bibliography using the author's last name, his first name and the title of the book. This information may be sufficient to tell whether a reference has been used, or to locate the book in the library, but it is not sufficient if one wants to buy the book. Obviously, one must know the publisher and place of publication. To evaluate the source of information, the date of writing must be known. For example, if the child says that a weather report in a newspaper predicted rain, he must be aware of the date this was printed. Children can understand that their height and weight will not always be the same, and that their age changes. Thus, what is true at one time may not be true at another.

▶ Outlining the topic

After he collects the information from the various sources he wants to use, he must make an outline of the major facts pertaining to his topic. He can then develop his paper in paragraph form. The first draft should be concerned with the expression of ideas. Then it can be corrected for vocabulary and sentence structure as well as punctuation, spelling and style. The footnotes and documentation should be written near the sentence to which it refers in the first rough draft. When the paper is re-written, this information can be placed in the proper place, after being verified for accuracy.

STEPS IN COMPLETING A RESEARCH PAPER

I. *Identification of the Problem*
   A. Is it a problem which interests me?
   B. Is the problem worth considering?
   C. Do I have adequate background to tackle the problem?
   D. Can I state the problem clearly and simply?
   E. Can I limit the problem so that I can realistically hope to solve it?

II. *Comparison of the Problem with Past Experiences*
   A. What do I already know about the problem?
   B. What can I learn from others about the problem?
   C. What resources are available to aid me in shedding light upon the problem?
   D. Do I have the skills necessary to use these resources?
      1. Can I locate information?
      2. Can I select information which relates to the problem?
      3. Can I evaluate the validity of information?
      4. Can I organize information into useable form?
      6. Do I know how to record my sources of information?

III. *Solution of the Problem*
   A. Do I have enough information to arrive at a satisfactory conclusion?
   B. What form does the solution take?
   C. Did I use a rational, reflective approach to the solution?

IV. *Writing the Paper*
   A. Is there a specific format to be followed in writing the paper?
   B. Should a rough draft be written first?
   C. Have I observed rules of good grammar, punctuation, and spelling?
   D. Have I documented my sources adequately?
   E. Does my paper make sense when read by someone else?

Research can be carried on by a whole class, by committees, and by individuals. The information can be presented in many different ways besides the ordinary oral or written report. Information can be illustrated by maps or pictures; it may be presented in the form of a play, television report, panel, debate or travelogue. It is important to use both primary and secondary sources. Science projects should include experiments. Interviews with authorities or people actively engaged in the field of research can make the information more significant. Trips to the source of information can enliven the study. When studying about the weather, students might visit, for example, a weather station to see how information is obtained and used to make up the weather report that appears in a newspaper or is given over the radio or television. The unit or topic of research can be correlated with most subjects in an integrated classroom. The research skills can be a part of any subject area and should be taught on each level with material that the individual can read and comprehend at the time. Suggestions for doing research in the area of "The Weather" will be given for elementary and secondary students to indicate the likeness and differences in doing research for various age groups.

A. A Sixth Grade Committee Studies Weather Prediction

Mr. McKenzie and his sixth grade class had just completed a three-day series of activities which served to orient them to a study of weather and climate. Several instructional films and filmstrips had been viewed. Mr. McKenzie had placed a series of photographs depicting several types of weather on the science bulletin board with a thought-provoking "Do *you* know what is taking place?" written below them. Several lively discussions were also held during which the class talked informally about their own experiences with weather, what it meant to them, and what types of things about weather and climate appeared to be important as well as interesting. It had also been possible for them to view a 30-minute television lesson which developed the basic scientific theories behind the world's major wind systems, opening up new areas of interest to them.

▶ Preparing the class list

The class was now ready to begin planning in earnest for a unit study which would last for several weeks. After careful consideration, they decided that the theme of their unit would be "How Weather Affects Man," and under the guidance of Mr. McKenzie they began to list the questions and problems which they felt would be important parts of the unit. These were listed on the chalkboard as they were suggested. Soon it was evident that many areas were of concern to the group. Among their questions were the following:

1. How do winds affect weather around the world?
2. How are storms created?
3. In what ways do clouds affect weather?
4. What are the different forms of precipitation, and how are they created?
5. How has man been able to put weather to work for him?
6. In what ways does weather affect the daily lives of people around the world?
7. What are the functions of the weather bureau?
8. How is weather predicted?
9. What instruments are used to predict weather?
10. What are weather maps and how are they used?

▶ Forming investigating committees

As the group began to discuss the questions, it became apparent that they had many interests. Mr. McKenzie suggested that the needed information might be gathered more thoroughly if the members of the class formed committees centered on their personal interests. Four boys with similar interests decided to work together as a committee to study the weather bureau and its role in the prediction of weather. Since Mr. McKenzie had given them time to organize their cooperative study, they took advantage of this opportunity to do several things. First of all, it was necessary for them to be sure of exactly what they wanted to find out. Following Mr. McKenzie's advice, they began to make a list of the specific questions which would be answered. Out of the two original questions, "What are the functions of the weather bureau?" and "How is weather predicted?", they were able to develop a number of subordinate questions. It became evident, however, that before their list of specific questions could be completed, they had to know something about the weather bureau and weather forecasting. By referring to their science textbooks, they realized that several important facets of both topics would have been missed simply because the students were not totally aware of the nature of their problems. After referring to their textbooks and several supplementary books available in the classroom, they were able to complete their list of questions. These questions, shown below, served as the basis for the various committee activities which followed.

Main Question: What are the functions of the weather bureau?

Subordinate Questions: Who works at the weather bureau?

How do weather bureau employees learn about weather around the nation?

What are some of the technical words used by weathermen? What do they mean?

What are the various jobs performed by the weathermen?

What kinds of equipment must they learn to operate?

How is weather information communicated to the people who need it?

Main Question: How is weather predicted?

Subordinate Questions: How did people predict weather in the past?

What facts must a weatherman know in order to predict or forecast the weather?

How accurate are the weather bureau's predictions?

What kinds of records of weather are kept?

▶ Methods for obtaining reference material

The next problem which the group discussed was the way in which they would go about obtaining the answers to their questions. They felt that the wisest thing to do would be to list the sources at their disposal and then decide which ones would be consulted and for what types of information. Among the resources on their list were the following: encyclopedias, tradebooks on weather, magazine articles, pamphlets, a trip to the weather bureau, a series of experiments which might help them to understand the problems of weather prediction.

After considering the specific questions which were to be answered, and drawing up a tentative list of resources, the group visited the school library as the first step in their research work.

48

Since several sets of encyclopedias were available, these were consulted initially. Mr. McKenzie had discussed encyclopedias several times with the class, and the boys knew that they contained articles written by authorities in various fields, and that the information which they contained was usually very factual. The encyclopedias were able to help them in several ways. A very complete section on the history of weather forecasting told them of the many superstitions surrounding weather, and pointed out that several of the old mariners' observations had some basis in fact. They were also able to obtain some very interesting information on the organization of the weather bureau itself, the responsibilities of the employees, and the equipment used to observe and record weather data.

▶ Dividing research tastes

At this stage in the project, the boys decided to divide the topic into four areas, since it was becoming obvious that there existed a great deal of information which would be best handled by individuals during the research stage. Later on, after all desired information had been gathered, they could meet again to organize the various parts of the topic into a comprehensive report which could be presented to the class. Thus, the four boys—Lance, Tom, Bob, and Bill—agreed to the following division of the topic:

Lance	*Tom*
Who works at the weather bureau?	What kinds of equipment must weathermen learn to operate?
How do weather bureau employees learn about weather around the nation?	What are some of the technical terms used by weathermen? What do they mean?
What are the various jobs performed by the weathermen?	How is weather information communicated to people who need it?

Bob	*Bill*
How did people predict weather in the past?	How accurate are the weather bureau's predictions?
What facts must a weatherman know in order to predict or forecast the weather?	What kinds of records of weather are kept?

The group continued to work in the library for some time, mak-

49

ing use of the various specialized trade and technical books available there. These were obtained in two ways: the school librarian was asked to suggest any resources which might help, and then, the boys made use of the card catalog which they had talked about during class with Mr. McKenzie. The school librarian was able to make several very practical suggestions. She pointed out several recent articles in magazines to which the library subscribed, brought out a new book on weather which was in the process of being catalogued and supplied several pamphlets, one of which was a government publication on the requirements for employment with the weather bureau. The card catalog was consulted under several headings—weather, storms, weather bureau, weather forecasting, etc. It became evident that most sources would be found under "weather," since most of the other subjects were cross-references to the "weather" topic.

Working with the information obtained from encyclopedias, a government pamphlet, and several books on weather, Lance was able to develop a more comprehensive outline of the types and duties of weather bureau employees and to ascertain in general the methods by which weather information was gathered. Tom already knew of several types of equipment used by weathermen. His list contained the centigrade and fahrenheit thermometer, aneroid barometer, anemometer, and hygrometer. He had also been introduced to a number of rather technical terms including mean temperature, Beaufort scale, absolute and relative humidity, precipitation, warm front, occluded front, cold front, and stationary front. As yet, he had not been able to obtain any information on the ways in which weather information was communicated to people in various parts of the country.

Bob had already found much information about weather prediction in the past, but was still able to add to this because he had come across a book which covered the history of weather prediction very thoroughly. It was written by a scientist who had at one time worked for the weather bureau and was now teaching the science of weather—meteorology—at a large university. Bob knew this from the author's description, carried on the title page of the book. Another book located in the library provided Bob with some information about air masses, fronts, and precipitation, as they relate to forecasting.

Bill was not very successful in discovering information concerning the accuracy of weather predictions, and thus, decided that further resources would have to be consulted. He considered several ideas, including an examination of the weather reports printed in a local paper over the past month and a comparison with the actual weather during the same time. He also felt that it would be possible to spend some time during the next week comparing the actual weather with that predicted in the weather forecast.

He found several references to records of weather information, particularly to weather maps, as ways of recording weather. He wondered how these maps were sent around the country, how they were made, and how often they were changed. This type of information was not available to him in the school library.

▶ *Comparing progress during individual research*

The four boys met again to compare the notes they had taken. After some discussion, they agreed that the next step in their research would be to make use of the public library which contained many special volumes on weather as well as standard reference works not contained in the school library. It was felt that each of them could gain further insight into the questions which faced them if more comprehensive resources were used at this point.

A short meeting with the librarian opened up several possibilities for the group. She assisted them by indicating a number of topical headings in the card catalog which contained books about weather. There were also a number of special references in the reference room including a science encyclopedia and several science journals which were written for students. The boys learned to locate these sources and to use them. They found that their previous instruction in class during which they had learned to use the *Readers' Guide*, cross-indexes, and cross references speeded up their work considerably.

They were also introduced to the pamphlet file maintained by the library. Under the heading of "Weather" they were able to locate several pamphlets including one which discussed the problem of accuracy in weather prediction and another which suggested

51

how amateurs could forecast weather by noting the humidity, air pressure, and wind direction.

During the trip to the library, each member of the group was able to add to his information because of the new and more specialized sources available to him. Lance found one reference on the use of the teletype for distributing weather forecasts. This source indicated that police departments throughout the state were kept abreast of the weather by means of the teletype. This suggested to him that a visit to police headquarters might enable him to see the teletype in action. Bob was able to gather a great deal of information about forecasting, by both professionals and amateurs, and felt that he would now be able to attempt some forecasting on his own.

Bill was not able to obtain any information concerning the accuracy of weather bureau forecasts. He felt that his own experimentation might shed some light on the problem, and in addition, now planned to talk with the weatherman at the local weather bureau, since one of the pamphlets indicated that the weather bureau did maintain records of the accuracy of their predictions.

Tom obtained a book written for children which contained an entire chapter about the construction of home-made weather instruments. Included were plans for the construction of a paper-cup anemometer, a wind-vane, a wind sock, and both water and air thermometers. In addition there were several types of barometers and a horse-hair hygrometer. He copied the plans for several of these, since he planned to construct them. He and Bill planned to use them in their own forecasting of weather, and believed that they would be useful in the class presentation.

A field trip to the local weather bureau was arranged next. A telephone call was made to the meteorologist who set a time when the boys would be able to meet with him at the weather bureau. On arrival they interviewed him, asking a number of questions which they had drawn up earlier. Lance was able to find out how weather maps were reproduced electronically throughout the country. In fact, the meteorologist presented him with one from the previous day and showed him how to interpret it.

Bill finally was able to view the records kept by the bureau over a period of time and obtained enough information to enable him to report to the class on the accuracy of weather prediction. Tom found the meterologist very willing to show him the various types of instruments used to obtain weather information. Of course, much of the equipment was on the roof of the building, but Tom was able to view the various dials which pointed out wind direction, speed. His work with the models had given him an idea of the equipment on the roof, so he was able to understand the explanations given about such instruments as the anemometer and the wind vane.

▶ Assimilating individual research material

The boys agreed that they had enough information to write a report and to present it before the class. Each of them had taken notes on 5 x 8 cards and met to arrange them, in order to write the report. They decided that each would write a part of the report and that the four parts would be joined together in a notebook. Accompanying the written material was an appendix which contained the weather map, pictures of weather instruments, and a sample of the teletyped weather forecast presented to the group by the local police. The finished report contained the following parts:

1. Title Page. (This included the title of the report, the names of the four writers, and the date.)
2. Table of Contents. (The boys decided to turn each of their questions into statements from which sub-titles could be developed. Thus, "How accurate are the weather bureau's predictions?" became "The accuracy of weather bureau predictions.")

Sample

Workers at the Weather Bureau. 1
Responsibilities of the Weathermen. 3
Equipment used by Weathermen. 6

3. Running Text. (A rough copy was written and reviewed for grammar, punctuation, and sense. This was recopied according to the format suggested by Mr. McKenzie.)
4. Bibliography. (All pamphlets, books, and other sources used in the formulation of the report were listed alphabetically by author in the form illustrated below: Frasier, George W., and others, *Science Problems 6*, Syracuse: L. W. Singer Co., 1962.)
5. Appendix.
   A. Weather Map
   B. Teletyped Weather Forecasts
   C. Illustrations of Weather Instruments

After the report was completed and checked, it was contributed to the collection which the class had been making for reference purposes. The oral report made by the group was based on the material contained in the written report. Each of the four boys developed a series of note cards which helped him keep his ideas in sequence. Suggestions for effective oral presentations had been given by Mr. McKenzie. These were kept in mind during the presentation. The plan for presentation for the oral talks is outlined below:

1. Introduction of the topic.
2. Presentation of findings.
   a. The weather bureau and its functions.
   b. The prediction of weather.
3. Demonstration of weather instruments.
4. Question and answer period.

B. A Ninth Grader Studies Rainmaking

Jack Carter's interest in rainmaking began during a unit concerned with weather and climate which was a part of the ninth grade general science curriculum. Miss Ryan, the general science teacher, had worked with the entire class of advanced students for several weeks during which a number of topics of general interest had been broached. In order to develop a broad basis for understanding, the scientific phenomena involved in the formation of weather and climate had been discussed, as well as the social implications of these natural forces at work. Such diverse areas of concern as cloud formations, wind systems, and weather prediction were examined. Several films and filmstrips had been viewed, and the general survey culminated by a visit to the weather bureau to witness modern techniques in weather forecasting.

▶ Initial class discussion

At this point, Miss Ryan mentioned to the class that each student would now have the opportunity to do some research in depth on a topic which interested them and which had some relationship

54

to the unit. She began by reviewing with the group the various topics which they had studied, following the review with a discussion of special interests held by students. When she was satisfied that all students had identified a topic which interested them, she then reviewed the steps that are usually followed in research and reference work of the type that was to be done. Since these steps were part of a format which had been agreed upon by the faculty, she had created a transparency which was now projected upon the screen for purposes of the review.

▶ Identifying the problem

Jack's attention was first called to rainmaking by a treatment which consisted of two paragraphs in his basic textbook. During a discussion of rain and snow, the authors referred to the fact that modern rainmakers usually attempt to make nuclei around which raindrops may form, and that pellets of dry ice (solid carbon dioxide) may be used for this purpose. However, the textual treatment was very sparse, and served, in fact, to whet Jack's appetite for more information. In a supplementary textbook he found that rain making is often accomplished by means of a method referred to as "cloud seeding," and that silver iodide particles are usually employed to form the needed nuclei. He was also fascinated by a discussion of the possibilities which rainmaking offered to improve living conditions, agriculture and water supplies for drinking. Thus, his curiosity began to grow even more.

However, at this point, he realized that before any serious research could be made, it would be necessary to state his problem in such a way that it would be easy to understand. He had to be sure that he could cope with it and that he knew exactly what he was looking for. Clearly, he did not as yet have sufficient information to delimit his problem very succinctly. This realization led him to several simplified general encyclopedias available in the school library. He used them since he realized that they would aid him in his attempt to develop the basic understandings needed for a comprehensive view of his problem.

He next had to consider some additional factors which would

affect the depth and scope of his problem. Miss Ryan had indicated that the results of the research should be written according to standard format and should not exceed fifteen pages in length, including bibliography, and that papers would be due in three weeks. Jack also realized that he knew very little about the topic, and thus, should not attempt to do too much. Miss Ryan had reminded the class that one of the major problems met by students doing research is that they attempt to do more than can be considered realistic in light of circumstances. After a consideration of the limitations under which he would be working and some reflection upon the preliminary information gathered from textbooks and simplified encyclopedias, Jack was able to frame a statement which included the nucleus of his working outline:

Rainmaking Today

1. How did modern rainmaking originate?
2. What methods are used to produce rain?
3. How successful have these methods been?
4. What possibilities do scientists see for the future in rainmaking?

After checking with Miss Ryan, Jack felt that he was ready to begin the information-gathering process. He had been careful to discuss with Miss Ryan his concern as to whether or not his problem was a realistic one in terms of the resources at his disposal and the other limiting factors within which he had to work.

Jack made a list of the *places* to which he could go for further information. These included the school library, the local public library, a nearby office of the Weather Bureau, and a neighboring university, whose library he had obtained permission to use through Miss Ryan. He then made a list of the types of resources which promised to be of assistance. This list included the following: adult general encyclopedias, journals and newspapers, scientific encyclopedias, pamphlets, scientific tradebooks, personal interviews.

Another problem that had to be faced at this time was the fact that information concerning rainmaking might be found under several headings. He wanted to be sure that no important sources would be missed, so he made a list of headings under which he might possibly find information related to the topic. These included: rainmaking, cloud seeding, cloud physics, weather control. Each of these had been suggested by his preliminary reading.

He was now ready to go ahead with the information-gathering process. Jack had decided to use note cards (5 x 8 lined) on which to record relevant information. He rejected the smaller 3 x 5 cards since they rarely prove adequate in size for this type of task. He developed a coding system which enabled him to identify each card immediately and to place it within his previously framed set of questions.

Origin of Rainmaking .... I.
    Sub-Topics .... A, B, C, etc.
      Details .... 1, 2, 3, etc.
Methods of Rainmaking .... II.
Success of Rainmaking .... III.
Future Possibilities .... IV.

Thus, a card containing notes referring to cloud seeding by means of a sodium chloride bomb released from an aircraft over Africa might be keyed as follows:

$$II - C - 2$$
II (Methods of Rainmaking)
C (Use of sodium chloride)
2 (Application from aircraft)

With such a coding system, organization of notes at a later date would be a relatively simple matter, particularly if a large number of notes were required.

Jack found that a survey of general, adult-level encyclopedias contributed very little to what he already knew. His next step was to consult a technical and scientific encyclopedia with a very informative article under the topic, "Cloud Physics." One section of the article in particular gave him an explanation of "cloud seeding," although he had to review carefully the explanation concerning the formation of rain which preceded the section with which he was concerned. He also learned that several types of rainmaking had been attempted. These included the use of dry ice (carbon dioxide in solid form), water drops, dust particles, sodium chloride, and silver iodide, all dropped into clouds from aircraft. In addition, mention was made of attempts to generate ice crystals near the windward side of a mountain where ascending damp air might produce snow on the leeward side. This snow, upon reaching the ground, could then be recovered as run-off water. He also came upon a description of silver iodide generators which could be aimed

57

upward toward clouds to perform the same task as that of the aircraft.

Another paragraph indicated that rainmaking experiments were being carried on in several countries including Australia, Canada, the United States and East Africa, as well as the Caribbean area. Although some experiments resulted in marked increases in rainfall, the results were not yet conclusive.

Jack was now making significant progress. Although he knew little as yet about the history of rainmaking, it was fast becoming evident that although several methods had been developed, none appeared to be an unqualified success. There was reason, however, to be optimistic about future success and application of rainmaking in many ways.

On checking the copyright date of the encyclopedia, he was assured that the article was rather up-to-date. Yet, several problems faced him. Could there have been any advances in rainmaking since the article was written? What specific information might he obtain about the methods described in the article? Where would he be able to delve into the history of modern scientific rainmaking? How do scientists determine whether or not the rainmaking attempts have been successful? Where have the successes occurred? What further information might he obtain concerning possible applications of rainmaking?

► Analyzing and selecting research material

Clearly, the next step was to go to more specific, yet authoritative and timely sources. These would include books written by scientists working in the field; articles in scientific journals as well as in newspapers and in popular periodicals; and pamphlets distributed by scientific organizations as well as the weather bureau. A telephone call to the weather bureau produced a promise to send a bibliography of government materials available on the subject. Such documents could either be sent for, if necessary, or sought at the local public library in the pamphlet file.

A check with the *Readers' Guide to Periodical Literature* for the past several years produced the following articles which Jack had to consider.

Rainmaking

1. Randomized cloud seeding in Santa Barbara J. Neyman and others il Science 131:1073-8 Ap 15 '60.
2. Summer clouds seeded Sci. N.L. 75:86 F 7 '59.
3. Up over down under: New South Wales Newsweek 56:52 S 5 '60.

Weather Control

4. Can we change the weather? D. Cohen il Sci Digest 52:70-82, N '62.
5. Weather control: use of asphalt costings to tap solar energy J. F. Black il Science 139:226-7 Ja 18 '63.

Cloud Physics

6. Ice nuclei from the ocean Sci. N.L. 72:326 My 21 '60.

Articles one and two appeared to relate to the cloud-seeding process, while article three seemed to relate to rainmaking in Australia, a country which Jack already knew, had experimented in the field. Jack was not sure about article four, but decided that it might shed some light on future possibilities for rainmaking. Article five appeared to have no relationship and was disregarded, although six was interesting to Jack since it appeared to be concerned with the physical explanation of seeding.

Each article was examined carefully. In addition to the information presented, Jack had to consider the qualifications of the writers, the type of journal or magazine in which the article appeared, and the relationship of the new material to what he had already uncovered. When he was satisfied that the assertions made by an article could be accepted as authoritative, he went ahead with his note-taking procedure.

It became apparent to him later that none of the articles were able to shed any light upon several of his questions. Thus, he would have to seek more comprehensive sources from the card catalog. He again looked under the various headings which he had listed earlier, and was able to locate a number of sources which appeared to be relevant. Several of these are listed below:

Critchfield, Howard J., *General Climatology,* Englewood Cliffs: Prentice-Hall, 1960.

Koeppe, Clarence E. and George C. DeLong, *Weather and Climate,* New York: McGraw-Hill Book Co., 1958.

Mason, B. J., *Clouds, Rain, and Rainmaking,* London: Cambridge University Press, 1962.

Orr, Clyde Jr., *Between Earth and Space,* New York: Macmillan, 1959.

Sutton, O. G., *The Challenge of the Atmosphere*, New York: Harper and Brothers, 1961.

Several questions now presented themselves to Jack. Which of the books listed in the catalog under "Weather" actually contained information about rainmaking? From which could he expect to obtain up-to-date information? How could he be sure that the information would be authoritative?

Skillful use of the catalog cards themselves gave Jack several of the answers which he was seeking. Obviously, the titles all indicated to him the possibility that the books would contain information concerning rainmaking, although it would be necessary in some cases to refer to the indexes of the books themselves to be certain. In the case of the book *Clouds, Rain, and Rainmaking*, the title provides a most obvious clue. In some cases it was possible to ascertain the fact that rainmaking was included by consulting the brief description reproduced on the catalog card.

▶ Determining timeliness of material

The determination of the timeliness of information included several considerations. First of all, the copyright date of each publication gave Jack a rough estimate of the recency of the information. However, Jack was able to make a more careful determination in several cases by referring to the footnotes contained in several books. Bibliographies also aided in the determination of time of publication, since bibliographical information includes the use of such dates. Jack also referred carefully to the running text in which the experiments described were often identified by the use of place-names and dates.

▶ Determining author's authority

Jack realized that one way of assuring himself that the information contained in books on the subject of rainmaking was authoritative was to check the qualifications of the author. In each of the above cases, it was possible to ascertain such qualifications simply by referring to the descriptive material contained on the book jackets. Jack was particularly interested in the *education, experience* and *achievements* of each author—and found, to his satisfaction, that all of the subject authors could be considered authoritative.

The recording of information was then accomplished by means of note-taking, using 5 x 8 cards coded and arranged as in the example below:

III-A-1   Mason, B. J.
                            Clouds, Rain and Rainmaking
                            London: Cambridge U. Press, 1962.

Conditions for Successful Cloud Seeding

pp. 98-99   1. 100% chance of precipitation if cloud summit temperatures −7 degrees or colder.
            2. Cloud depth is an important factor.
            3. Life-time of cloud.

▶ Preparing a working outline

When Jack had satisfied himself that all readily available sources such as journals, pamphlets, encyclopedias, textbooks, and tradebooks had been checked and relevant information properly noted, he was ready to organize his material into a usable form. This enabled him to write a rough draft of his research paper. Below is an outline of the format which Jack used for his paper—one which had been suggested by Miss Ryan.

     I. Statement of the Problem
    II. Justification of the Topic
  III. Review of the Literature
  IV. Analysis of the Literature
     V. Conclusions
   VI. Appendix
  VII. Bibliography

▶ Preparing the rough draft

As he prepared to write his rough draft, Jack reviewed the notes he had taken and began to draw the conclusions which he felt were appropriate. The statement of his problem was very easily formulated since he had taken care to consider this carefully before beginning to gather information. He felt that the problem was justified for several reasons: (1) it related to the unit of study in science, (2) it interested him personally, and (3) his research told him that rainmaking appeared to hold promise for future weather control. In his review of the literature, he used his note cards to develop a logical, sequential description of information which he had found to be related to his major questions: (How did modern rainmaking originate? What methods are used to produce rain? How successful have these methods been? What possibilities do scientists see for the future in rainmaking?) He was then able to analyze his findings and reach a number of conclusions concerning his original questions. In his appendix, he included several diagrams which illustrated various cloud-seeding procedures, taking care to label each illustration with a title and a capital letter which could be used for identification when referred to in the text. The bibliography was constructed according to school requirements. In this case two separate sections were created, one which included articles from journals and periodicals and another which contained textbooks and tradebooks.

Examples from each section are included below:

Articles

Mason, B. J., "The Physics of Rain-Making," *Discovery*, 16:461, November, 1955.

Orville, Howard T., "Weather Made to Order," *Colliers*, 133:25, May 28, 1954.

Neyman, J. et al., "Randomized Cloud Seeding in Santa Barbara," *Science*, 131:1073-8, April 15, 1960.

Books and Pamphlets

Bush, George L. and Will S. Thompson, *Worlds of Science*, New York: American Book Co., 1959.

Mason, B. J., *Clouds, Rain, and Rainmaking*, London: Cambridge University Press, 1962.

McGraw-Hill Encyclopedia of Science and Technology, New York: McGraw-Hill, 1960 (Volume 3).

The rough draft was reviewed for clarity of thought and expression, correct grammar and punctuation, and accuracy of spelling. When Jack was satisfied that this represented his best efforts, he recopied it—keeping a carbon for himself and giving the original to Miss Ryan.